"We don't meet people
by accident.
They are meant
to cross our path
For a Reason."

Printed in Great Britain
by Amazon

43269330R00030